HOUSES AND HOMES

Poetry

Selected by
Robert Hull

Illustrated by
Annabel Spenceley

Wayland

Thematic Poetry

Animal Poetry
Christmas Poetry
Day and Night Poetry
Food Poetry
Green Poetry
Houses and Homes Poetry
Science Poetry
Sea Poetry

Series editor: Catherine Ellis
Editor: Susannah Foreman
Designer: Derek Lee

First published in 1992 by
Wayland (Publishers) Ltd
61 Western Road, Hove
East Sussex BN3 1JD, England

**British Library Cataloguing in
Publication Data**
Houses and Homes Poetry. —
   (Thematic Poetry Series)
   I. Hull, Robert   II. Spenceley,
   Annabel   III. Series
   821.008
ISBN 0-7502-0618-7

Picture Acknowledgements

The publishers would like to thank the
following for allowing their illustrations to
be reproduced in this book: the Hutchison
Library 31, 37, 44; Life File 40; Christine
Osborne 22; Oxford Scientific Films 11, 12,
21; Reflections (Jennie Woodcock) 24, 32,
43; Tony Stone Worldwide *back cover*, 5,
7, 8, 18; Zefa *front cover*, 15, 16, 26, 34, 38.

Acknowledgements

For permission to reprint copyright material the
publishers gratefully acknowledge the following:
Andre Deutsch Ltd. for 'The People Upstairs' by
Ogden Nash, from *I Wouldn't Have Missed It*; Gina
Douthwaite for 'Millionaire's Mansion'; Katherine
Gallagher for 'Near Keith, South Australia'; Harper
Collins Publishers for 'Old Poem', trans. by Arthur
Waley, from *Chinese Poems*; Deborah Hayman for
'Going to Bed'; David Higham Associates for 'Song of
the Battery Hen' by Edwin Brock; Wes Magee for
'the electronic house'; The National Exhibition of
Children's Art for 'Bedroom for Rent' by Nick Ashby,
from *The Cadbury Fourth Book of Children's Poetry*;
'Benediction for the Tent' trans. by C. R. Bawden
from *The Penguin Book of Oral Poetry* ed. by Ruth
Finnegan (Allen Lane, 1978), copyright © Ruth
Finnegan, 1978, reproduced by permission of
Penguin Books Ltd.; 'Guns' (p123) from *Modern
Poetry of the Arab World* (1986) trans. and ed. by
Abdullah al-Udhari, translation copyright © Abdullah
Al-Udhari, 1986, reproduced by permission of
Penguin Books Ltd; 'An Unguarded House' by
Julianus, trans. by W. S. Merwin from *The Greek
Anthology* ed. Peter Jay (Allen Lane, 1973) copyright
© Peter Jay, 1973, reproduced by permission of
Penguin Books Ltd; 'The Mother's Song' trans. by
Peter Freuchen, from *Book of the Eskimos*, reprinted
by permission of the Peters Fraser & Dunlop Group
Ltd; 'Dancing Teepees' by Calvin O'John, from
Whispering Wind by Terry Allen. Copyright © 1972
Institute of American Indian Arts. By permission of
Doubleday, a division of Bantam Doubleday Dell
Publishing Group, Inc.: 'I know some lonely houses'
from *The Complete Poems of Emily Dickinson* (Little
Brown & Co); Heinemann Ltd for Rachel Fields'
'Houses' from *Taxis and Toadstools*; 'winter rain'
from *The Orange Balloon* (Here Press) copyright ©
1980 Penny Harter, and 'grandmother's mirror' from
In the Broken Curve (Burnt Lake Press) copyright ©
1984 Penny Harter.
Typeset by Dorchester Typesetting Group Ltd, England
Printed in Italy by G. Canale & C.S.p.A., Turin

Contents

Introduction

When it's cheerful and peaceful, home is a good place to be. When it's in a beautiful place too, even better: you might envy the children in the poem 'Dancing Teepees', who play with bows and arrows on the banks of Cripple Creek, high up in the Rocky Mountains. In his poem, nine-year-old Nick Ashby wants to rent his bedroom for a while. You might like to swap with a very rich person, and live in 'The Millionaire's Mansion' for a while.

Poets swap houses and homes in their heads, and imagine in their poems what it's like living somewhere else. One poem describes how the snail feels living in his shell-house: 'I am always at home', he says. Imagining isn't easy. It is difficult for people living in peaceful countries to imagine living where wars are fought. One poet, hearing 'the guns roar at dawn' describes how 'in an empty flat . . . the vase is shaking'. Another tells the grim story of a woman who has just lost her home through bombing.

We have included poems about such grim subjects, because poetry is about real life, not just about what's pretty or funny or nice. But life is beautiful and funny as well as grim, and there are poems here about such moments in our homes: a mother watching her little boy asleep, or the noise from the people upstairs, who 'go to the bathroom on roller-skates'.

There may be moments that happen in your home or in an imagined one – funny, serious, frightening, beautiful, strange moments – that you can write your own poems about. The king in his palace, the bees in the hive, Diogenes in his tub, stone-age people in their caves; there are hundreds of house poems waiting to be written. In the meantime, let your imagination enjoy living in these poems, these small buildings of words.

The Mother's Song

It is so still in the house,
There is a calm in the house;
The snowstorm wails out there,
And the dogs are rolled up with snouts under the tail.
My little boy is sleeping on the ledge,
On his back he lies, breathing through his open mouth.
His little stomach is bulging round –
Is it strange if I start to cry with joy?

ANON.
(Translated from the Inuit by Peter Freuchen)

Song of the Battery Hen

We can't grumble about accommodation:
we have a concrete floor that's
always dry, four walls that are
painted white, and a sheet-iron roof
the rain drums on. A fan blows warm air
beneath our feet to disperse the smell
of chicken shit and, on dull days,
fluorescent lighting sees us.

You can tell me: if you come by
the North door, I am in the twelfth pen
of the left-hand side of the third row
from the floor; and in that pen
I am usually the middle one of three.
But even without directions, you'd
discover me. I have the same orange-
red comb, yellow beak and auburn
feathers, but as the door opens and you
hear above the electric fan a kind of
one-word wail, I am the one
who sounds loudest inside my head.

Listen. Outside this house there's an
orchard with small moss-green apple
trees; beyond that, two fields of
cabbages; then, on the far side of
the road, a broiler house. Listen:
one cockerel grows out of there, as
tall and proud as the first hour of sun.
Sometimes I stop calling with the others
to listen, and wonder if he hears me.

The next time you come here, look for me.
Notice the way I sound inside my head.
God made us all differently,
and blessed us with this expensive home.

EDWIN BROCK

9

An Unguarded House

Thieves, find some other house, worthy of robbing.
Sleepless poverty mounts guard over this one.

JULIANUS
(Translated from the Greek by W. S. Merwin)

Two Haiku

Winter rain
in our garage
the same stray cat

Grandmother's mirror –
age spots
the glass

PENNY HARTER

11

Old Poem

At fifteen I went with the army,
At fourscore I came home.
On the way I met a man from the village,
I asked him who there was at home.
'That over there is your house,
All covered over with trees and bushes.'
Rabbits had run in at the dog-hole,
Pheasants flew down from the beams of the roof.
In the courtyard was growing some wild grain;
And by the well, some wild mallows.
I'll boil the grain and make porridge,
I'll pluck the mallows and make soup.
Soup and porridge are both cooked,
But there is no-one to eat them with.
I went out and looked towards the east,
While tears fell and wetted my clothes.

ANON.
(Translated from the Chinese by Arthur Waley)

Living Tenderly

My body a rounded stone
with a pattern of smooth seams.
My head a short snake,
retractive, projective.
My legs come out of their sleeves
or shrink within,
and so does my chin.
My eyelids are quick clamps.

My back is my roof.
I am always at home.
I travel where my house walks.
It is a smooth stone.
It floats within the lake,
or rests in the dust.
My flesh lives tenderly
inside its bone.

MAY SWENSON

They are tracking down everything picturesque

they are tracking down everything picturesque

gentlemen came with portfolios and measuring rods
they measured the ground spread out their papers
workers shooed away the pigeons
ripped up the fences tore down the house
mixed lime in the garden
brought cement raised scaffolding
they are going to build an enormous apartment house

they are wrecking the beautiful houses one by one
the houses which nourished us since we were small
with their high ceilings lamps on the walls
trophies of folk architecture

they are tracking down everything picturesque
chasing it away to the upper part of the town
it expires like a revolution betrayed
in a little while it will not even exist in postcards
nor in the memory or souls of poor children

DINOS CHRISTIANOPOULOS
(Translated by Kimon Friar)

Bedroom for Rent

Bedroom for rent.
Windows big . . . includes spider's web.
Handmarks on walls with mixed felt tip colours.
Wool dangling from light bulb
makes very good Action Man swing.
Bed makes good car, ship, moon buggy, trampoline
and a warm snug place for the night.
Natives are friendly. Includes 2 gerbils
                            3 fish
                            1 dog

plus one free gift (Mum).
Accommodation is compact.
Bedroom for rent.
No reasonable offer refused.

NICK ASHBY (Aged 9)

19

I know some lonely Houses

I know some lonely Houses off the Road
A Robber'd like the look of –
Wooden barred,
And Windows hanging low,
Inviting to –
A Portico,
Where two could creep –
One – hand the Tools –
The other peep –
To make sure All's Asleep –
Old fashioned eyes –
Not easy to surprise!

How orderly the Kitchen'd look, by night,
With just a Clock –
But they could gag the Tick –
And Mice won't bark –
And so the Walls – don't tell –
None – will –

A pair of Spectacles ajar just stir –
An Almanac's aware –
Was it the Mat – winked,
Or a nervous star?
The Moon – slides down the stair,
To see who's there!

There's plunder – where –
Tankard, or Spoon –
Earring – or Stone –
A Watch – Some Ancient Brooch
To match the Grandmama –
Staid sleeping – there –

Day – rattles – too
Stealth's – slow –
The Sun has got as far
As the third Sycamore –
Screams Chanticleer –
'Who's there?'

And Echoes – Trains away,
Sneer – 'Where'!
While the old Couple, just
   astir,
Fancy the Sunrise – left the
   door ajar!

EMILY DICKINSON

Guns

The guns roar at dawn
And the sea enfolds the city like smoke
The guns roar at dawn
And the birds are frightened
Have the planes come?

In an empty flat
The plants are silent
The vase is shaking.

SA'DI YUSUF
(Translated from the Arabic by
Abdullah al-Udhari)

Going to Bed

Nobody's there,
On the stair,
On the landing,
In my bedroom,
In my bed.
That's what Dad said.

But if there's nobody there
What makes the stairs
Creak,
The doors slam,
The curtains shiver,
The shadows play?
That's what I say.

DEBORAH HAYMAN

25

Millionaire's Mansion

Shove through the shrubs in the graveyard,
carefully creep to the wall,
peep up on tiptoe, the rich man must not know
you're watching his *Midsummer Ball.*

Hear the Rolls Royce and Mercedes
swish down the sweep of the drive,
see chauffeurs dump very posh people,
spy shyly as grand guests arrive

like ladies who slither in silver
and strawberry-nosed men with names
like Ponsonby-Forbes or Hamilton-Orbes
or Smith-With-Some-Great-Claim-to-Fame.

Watch them parade like a circus
into the blue and white tent
which heaves in the breeze like all these marquees
that are hired at great expense.

Gaze as the evening gets darker,
as lights wink and blink at the sight
of salmon and jellies, and far-too-fat bellies
dancing away in the night.

Stay at the wall looking over.
There's no invitation for you.
Your name's on a tablet, not table
and ghost-crashing parties won't do!

GINA DOUTHWAITE

from *Benediction for the Tent*

We are erecting our palace
Upon the lofty plateau.

It is a sea-white palace
With its eight sides tied down
With eighty-two thongs.

Let us anoint its walls
With the ribs made of willow
From the northern Kanghai,
Fastened back and forth
With the spine-skin of an elk.

Let us anoint its roof-beams –
The roof-beams made of a tree
From the southern Kanghai,
The thongs made from the tail-hair
Of foal and colt.

Let us anoint the smoke-flap rope
Which struggles against the firmament.

Let us anoint the brazier for the fire,
With its four imperial pillars,
And its hoop of steel armour.

Let us offer up with loud voice,
A prayer for lasting good.

May this family
Gather all its beasts together outside,
Fill its tents with scholars,
Have a full set of carpets,
And plentiful food and fruit set out,
Be merry day and night,
Give good to all
Who pass by upwards,
And drink to all
Who pass by downwards,
Be too rich in foals to know them,
Be too rich in children to know them,
Make their koumiss-bag of elephant-skin,
Make their koumiss-paddle of sandal-wood,
Make their ornaments of magnolia-flowers,
Peg out a tethering-line sixty fathoms long,
With foals tethered to it like minnows.

May we humans
Flourish like the flowers of spring.

ANON.
(Translated from The Mongol by C.R. Bawden)

An Old Jamaican Woman Thinks about the Hereafter

What would I do forever in a big place, who
have lived all my life in a small island?
The same parish holds the cottage I was born in, all
my family, and the cool churchyard.
        I have looked
up at the stars from my front verandah and have been afraid
of their pathless distances. I have never flown
in the loud aircraft nor have I seen palaces,
so I would prefer not to be taken up high nor
rewarded with a large mansion.
        I would like
to remain half-drowsing through an evening light
watching bamboo trees sway and ruffle for a valley-wind,
to remember old times but not to live them again;
occasionally to have a good meal with no milk
nor honey for I don't like them, and now and again to walk
by the grey sea-beach with two old dogs and watch
men bring up their boats from the water.
        For all this,
for my hope of heaven, I am willing to forgive my debtors
and love my neighbour . . .
        although the wretch throws stones
at my white rooster and makes too much noise in her damn
    backyard.

A. L. HENDRICKS

Teevee

In the house
of Mr and Mrs Spouse
he and she
would watch teevee
and never a word
between them spoken
until the day
the set was broken.

Then, 'How do you do?'
said he to she,
'I don't believe
that we've met yet.
Spouse is my name.
What's yours?' he asked.

'Why, mine's the same!'
said she to he,
'Do you suppose that we could be – ?'

But the set came suddenly right about
and so they never did find out.

EVE MERRIAM

33

Dancing Teepees

Dancing teepees
High up in the Rocky Mountains
Dancing teepees
Dance on the grassy banks of Cripple Creek
With laughing fringes in the autumn sun.
Indian children
Play with bows and arrows
On the grassy banks of Cripple Creek.
Indian women
gather kindling to start an evening fire.
Dancing teepees
Dance against fire-lighted autumn trees.
Braves returning
Home from raiding,
Gallantly ride into camp
With horses, scalps and ornaments.
Dancing teepees
Sleep now on the grassy banks of Cripple Creek
High up in the Rocky Mountains.

CALVIN O'JOHN

Five Minutes After the Air Raid

In Pilsen,
Twenty-six Station Road,
she climbed to the Third Floor
up stairs which were all that was left
of the whole house,
she opened her door
full on to the sky,
stood gaping over the edge.

For this was the place
the world ended.

Then
she locked up carefully
lest someone steal
Sirius
or Aldebaran
from her kitchen,
went back downstairs
and settled herself
to wait
for the house to rise again
and for her husband to rise
   from the ashes
and for her children's hands
   and feet to be stuck back in place.

In the morning they found her
still as stone,
sparrows pecking her hands.

MIROSLAV HOLUB
(Translated from the
Czech by
George Theiner)

The People Upstairs

The people upstairs all practise ballet.
Their living room is a bowling alley.
Their bedroom is full of conducted tours.
Their radio is louder than yours.
They celebrate weekends all the week.
When they take a shower, your ceilings leak.
They try to get their parties to mix
By supplying their guests with Pogo sticks,
And when their orgy at last abates,
They go to the bathroom on roller-skates.
I might love the people upstairs wondrous
If instead of above us, they just lived under us.

OGDEN NASH

Near Keith, South Australia

I turn off the highway, follow signs
to a mud-brick cottage
tapestried with bearded grass, hollyhocks,
lavender, geraniums, pigface, sage.

My great-grandmother
who smoked a clay-pipe and bore eight children
lived like this, within bowed walls,
a track up to the door.

Today everything's locked, the single window
rations light. I peer in, picture a family
here in two rooms, children taking turns
to move closer to the fire –

throwing on logs to break the frost
while parents hungered
for the promised good year.

KATHERINE GALLAGHER

the electronic house

cooker blanket
  toothbrush fire
iron light-bulb
  tv drier
fridge radio
  robot drill
crimper speaker
  kettle grill
slicer grinder
  meters fan
slide-projector
  deep-fry pan
vacuum-cleaner
  fuses shocks
freezer shaver
  junction-box
water-heater

  Christmas lamps
knife recorder
  cables amps
door-chimes organ
  infra-red
guitar video
  sunlamp bed
synthesizer
  night-light glow
cultivator
  stereo
calculator
  metronome
toaster Teasmade
  ohm sweet ohm

WES MAGEE

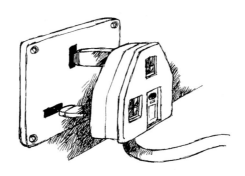

Houses

I like old houses best, don't you?
They never go cluttering up a view
With roofs too red and paint too new,
With doors too green and blinds too blue!
The old ones look as if they *grew,*
Their bricks may be dingy, their clapboards askew
From sitting so many seasons through,
But they've learned in a hundred years or two
Not to go cluttering up a view!

RACHEL FIELD

Biographies

Nick Ashby was nine, and a pupil at Cloudside Junior School in Nottingham, when he wrote this poem. It was published in 1986.

Edwin Brock was born in 1927. He was an editorial assistant, an advertising executive and a police constable before he became a full-time writer. He has written novels, plays and short stories as well as poetry.

Emily Dickinson (1830-1886) was one of the greatest American poets. She was very unlucky, because publishers thought her poems strange, and no one was willing to publish them until after her death. Even then, some of her words and punctuation were altered. She could say a tremendous amount in a few short lines.

Gina Douthwaite is a children's poet whose work has appeared in many anthologies and been broadcast on BBC Schools Radio. She runs workshops for children in schools and courses for adults, and works with children who have reading difficulties.

Rachel Field (1894-1942) was an American writer. She was born in New York, then lived in Massachusetts. She wrote children's poetry and stories, and novels for adults.

Katherine Gallagher is an Australian who has lived in London since 1979. She has published four books of poems. The most recent is *Fish-Rings on Water*. She often holds poetry workshops in schools.

Deborah Hayman was born in 1971, and is a student at the West Sussex Institute of Higher Education. 'Going to Bed' is her first published poem.

Penny Harter is an American haiku poet.

A. L. Hendricks was born in Jamaica in 1922. He was manager of the

Jamaica Broadcasting Corporation, and has published poetry, short stories and articles about literature.

Miroslav Holub is world-famous both as a scientist and as a poet. He was born in 1923 in Czechoslovakia, and lived through the Nazi occupation of his country. He did not start writing poetry until he was thirty.

Julianus, called Julianus of Egypt, was probably a Roman official who lived in Egypt in the fifth century AD; he wrote many of his short poems in Greek.

Wes Magee lives in Yorkshire. One of his children's poetry books, *Morning Break*, was voted one of the best children's books of 1989.

Eve Merriam was born in 1916. She has written fiction, plays, screen-plays, biographies and essays as well as numerous books of poetry, for both children and adults. She lives in New York.

The Mongol people of eastern Central Asia live in both China and what until recently was the USSR. Many of them are horse-riding nomads, tending their herds. Poetry is very important to them, and it is 'oral' – not written down but memorized and handed down by word of mouth.

Ogden Nash is perhaps the best-known writer of comic verse in the USA. He has been called the 'funniest poet this country has known'.

Calvin O'John is a writer from the Ute-Navajo Indian people.

Sa'di Yusuf was born in Basra, Iraq in 1934. After training to be a teacher, he left Iraq for Beirut, and in 1982 moved to Cyprus, where he now lives.

May Swenson was born in Utah, USA in 1917. Her parents were Swedish, and she has translated Swedish poetry into English. She has published many books of poems, including *Poems to Solve, More Poems to Solve* and *The Guess and Spell Colouring Book*.

Arthur Waley (1889-1966) was a translator of Chinese and Japanese literature. Many Western readers have come to love Chinese poetry through his work.

Index of first lines